WHALING
TOWN

WHALING TOWN

POEMS

DAVID PARKER ALLEN

GRAPHONICA

Published by Graphonica, Lake Bluff, IL
www.davidparkerallen.com

Edited and designed by Girl Friday Productions
www.girlfridayproductions.com

Cover design: Greg Mortimer
Project management: Emilie Sandoz-Voyer
Editorial production: Kylee Hayes
Image credits: cover © iStock/Basil Andreyev

ISBN (paperback): 979-8-9993789-0-3
ISBN (ebook): 979-8-9993789-1-0

Library of Congress Control Number: 2025916535

First edition

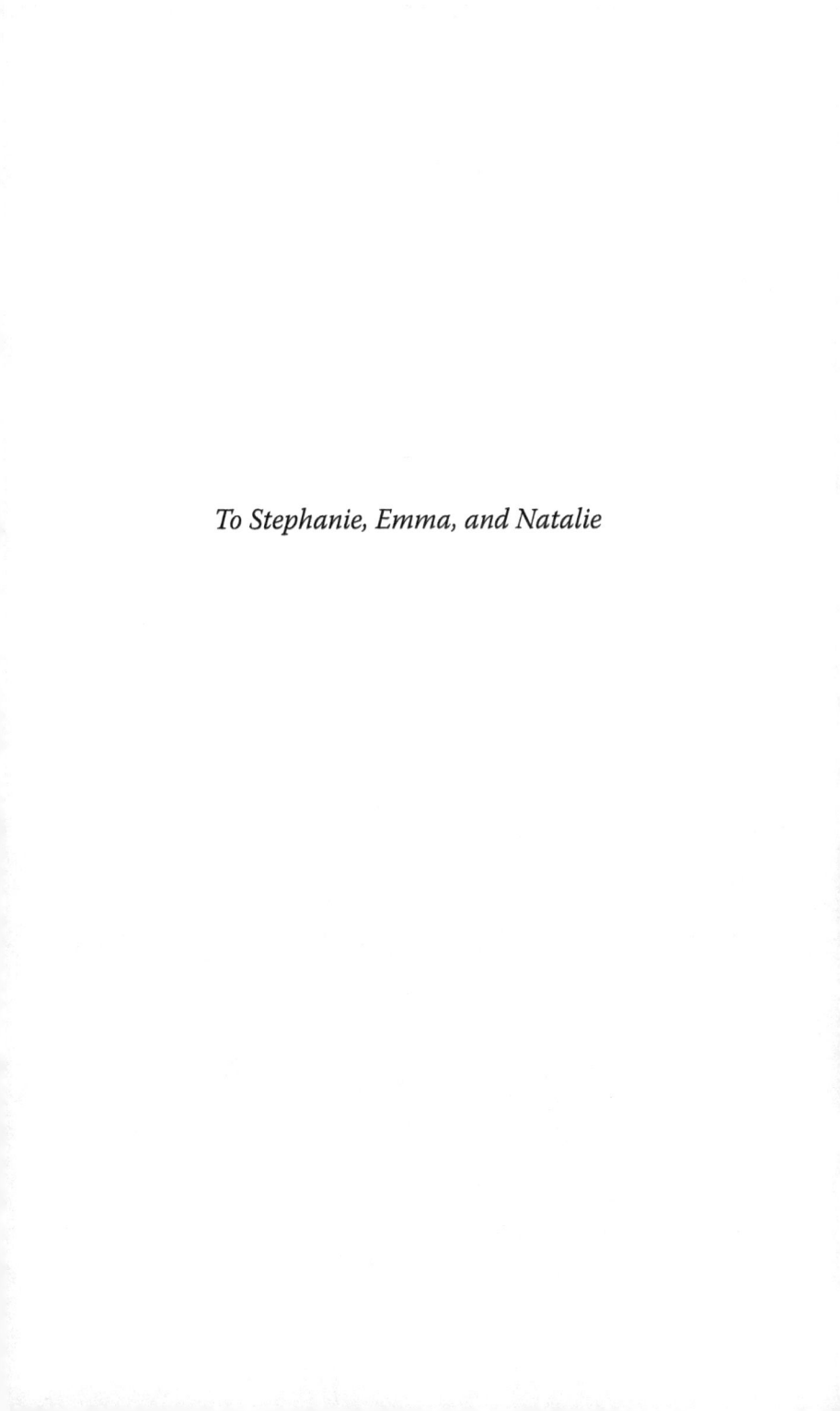

To Stephanie, Emma, and Natalie

POEMS

A Whisper from Gone 1
American Factoid 3

PART I.

Requiem in Manhattan 9
Under the L 11
Quantum Stranger 13
The Delta 14
In a Little Town in the USA 15
Meat Cooking in Selma 17
Derivatives of a Bob Dylan Love Song 19
Montana 22
Reuben at the Bluff 24
Beans and Meat 25
Mandalay 29
When I Walk into an Old Barn of Tools 31
Frontier Newspaper 32

PART II.

Whaling Town 37

PART III.

Staring Contest with a Blackbird 47
In the Dark Wood I Spotted 49
Nocturnal Mountain Road 51

Song for Charlie Patton 52
Over This Lonesome Field 54
When I Wet the Lips of Death 55
Roaring '20s 56
I See Headlights Coming 57
In the Din of the Plunging Breakers 59
Ocean Lung 61
The Autopsy of Oscar Parker 62
Birth of a Tragedy 64
Love Tape, Eject 66
Here in the Fjord, High in the Fjord 67
Fire and Ice 68
Daughter 70
Room 703 71
I Got You Babe 73
Thawing 76
I'll Meet You at the Swing 78
I Hope I Don't Expire Unexpected 80
Eat Your Heart Out 81

Acknowledgments 83
About the Author 87

POEMS

A Whisper from Gone

In my hands is a soft green book,
that smell of fading yellow pulp, copyright 1907.
There is a poem in it, 'Deep Down Things,'
after one called 'The Coming War.'
'The Coming War' foretells an Armageddon among nations,
seven years before WWI.
Rather prescient fellow, I'd say.

He wrote, "Nations will go down in slaughter. Ancient
    capitals burned."

WWI, then WWII. One Great War.
That great generation, my grandmother's,
    a whisper from gone.

No world war in the last eighty years, and sure, the rest-
    less are stirring,
but what catches my attention
as I turn its delicate pages
is a bending thick line in pencil down the side of a para-
    graph, just one.

Yes, it's another man's book.
'Mr. E. L. Ely. Nov. 1909,'

inscribed in that old-fashioned way.
But it gets to me for a second,
staring at the handwritten mark of another man's thoughts
from a hundred years ago, trying to speak to me now,
next to a marked paragraph with the line:

"Why are there no reformers fighting in the world today?"

I almost start to think deep about it,
but instead put the book down, giving pause,

thinking of my grandmother, who lived it,
remembering kissing her warm wet head,

"Honey, how are you?"
she said to me that day,
dying in my arms.

An angel on earth.

When people ask, "What was it like back then?"

That's what it was like.

American Factoid

I bought a dictionary.
A hard-bound, good old-fashioned *Webster's*.
At age fifty-three.
The clock is ticking.
Amazon delivered within three hours.
When I opened it, my wife looked at me funny.
It was that look.
I asked, "Want to go to bed?"
What do you think?

I opened the dictionary.
Not quite as good as an afternoon embrace,
but bible-thin paper has its benefits.
I picked a page, closed my eyes, and stuck my finger into
    the ink.

The word: Metempsychosis /me-tem-si-'kosis/ n (1561)—
    page 780 of the eleventh edition.
Never heard this word.
Says *Merriam*, "the passing of the soul at death into
    another body either human or animal."

My first thought was jumping into the body of a bear, no
    idea why.

I took another crack at it, flipped the pages,
and with closed eyes . . .

The word: Factoid /fak-toid/ n (1973).

"An invented fact believed to be true because it appears in
    print."

An *invented* fact *because it was in print*.
Hard to believe we put up with this.

1973, an interesting year.

My dad was staring at Russian tanks through army binoculars
on the Czech border near East Germany
while I played with a truck on a pile of dirt in West Germany
wearing diapers and a black beer shirt.
Dark Side of the Moon was released,
so was *Let's Get It On*.
Watergate was underway.
Vietnam was winding down. Yes, that Vietnam.
The one no one talks about anymore.

I'll tell you some facts about Vietnam.
My dad got orders to go to the jungle.
My grandfather was flying in combat,
dropping ammo to the grunts at Khe Sanh.
He's lying in the ground in Arlington with a DFC.
No wonder 'Factoid' was invented in 1973.

Which got me to thinking about stories.
The invented ones,
and the real ones, untold.

Like this one.

I wrote a song in Houston last week,
about a homeless man,
hustling.

'Homeless in Houston' it was called.

Didn't finish it.

His neighbors,
twelve feet down the way,
were a family with a box, a blanket, and two backpacks,
a big one and a small one.

It was a strung-out mom and a strung-out girl,
both blonde dreads.
Looked like they weren't from Houston.

I couldn't find the melody, I couldn't find the words,
and there was nothing more to say except
the title of that song.

PART I.

"Sisters and Brothers of America . . ."

Vivekananda
World Parliament of Religions
September 11, 1893

Requiem in Manhattan

In the middle of the night in Manhattan,
in a silent long hall, pulleys scrape
the pungent bowels of a building.

November 2, the Day of the Dead,
an October-warmth farewell,
cold drapes the sound of faint Cuban drums as I exit.
Box trucks pound and rattle over steel plates.
I walk past hushed Spanish accents,
and see St. Patrick's spires towering, white Gothic in the dark.
I am alone in the massive cathedral except a woman
        hunched tight in a ball,
praying, and I pick up a hymnal, tempting fate, and open
        to a page:

Santo.
San-to, San-to, San-tos el Se-nor,
Dios del U-ni-ver-so.

Now walking back down Fifty-Seventh,
the subway entrance, what's down there in the dark?
Descending, I feel heat,
the warmth of the tunnels in winter. Yes of course.
Then hot urine dank, and a banging in the caverns.

A body is lying far in the arches, almost naked,
and as I step close, I see dead asleep on the tile,
the subtropic bare skin of a man curled in Picasso's
blue pose, his calloused feet in black rubber shoes.

I walk up to him, so close I can see chalk dust in his beard,
then I turn back around.
Why am I not sitting down next to him, to look out for him,
or dropping an envelope in his sack?
Because I don't want to disturb him.
Or, maybe I'm disturbed with myself,
or with the cold hard tile
in the underground of this world.

Resurfacing,
the dark is losing its grip.
Garbage trucks accelerate.
Hydraulic brakes screech.
Glass bottles crash.
Silent stares of workers punch in.
And in the rumble over manholes,
the bustle of the morning is upon us.

Under the L

Under the L in Chicago
in a biting-cold wind, a white man
warms his hands inside a plastic bag
wrapped around a hot coffee.
Gloves he has made.

It is very early morning, in December.
He sits at a window seat
in a merciful warmth after a long night,
and through glass I see him exhale.

Above me the L,
a gestapo's whistle,
a rattle far away,
a gnash of steel,
a stampede of tonnage
conducting electrons and ions.

And if I put my bare hands on the rail of this dry ice-cold
    track
to stop this beastly train,
it will wheel its flying weight and cut my frozen fingers
    right off.

It is a beautiful day too.
A blue so blue.

Quantum Stranger

Listening to silence reminds me of a woman
I passed thirty seconds ago walking in O'Hare.
Her face middle age,
tangled and tender,
she has come to the edge of the world's horizon,
saying nothing, exhaling smoke, laughing.

They say quantum particles do this and that,
and it might be.
I feel the hard black rubber
of the escalator rail on her way down,
and see the steel rivet jaws fold,
and her tunnel vision in the revolving exit doors,
while she looks down for no reason
when she comes to meet the car on the curb.

I can see her staring out the passenger-seat window,
and the pink on her cheek,
and I want to paint her faraway face in the exact ten seconds
she is listening to the question "How was your day?"

I turn up 'So What' as I enter Terminal C,
and the world splits in two.

The Delta

I went to the Delta searching for seeds
where the great flood came.

I found it in dry dirt, on W. C. Handy's bench,
level with rust tracks and broken glass,
and in the juke's faint pulse, a sound
underwater and underground.

In a field next to the plantation is a hand-scratched grave
in the shape of a house, it reads,

'Harry Jones Is As Rest
Gone But Not Forgotton.'

In a Little Town in the USA

On a wall in a little town
in East Tennessee
hangs a sign: COFFEE.

Christ **O**ffers **F**orgiveness **F**or **E**veryone **E**verywhere.

. . . and a Hall of Fame picture of locals,
. . . and a country singer's autograph.

The gathering place of this town has chairs,
the ones from church basements,
with tennis balls punctured onto each leg
sliding on linoleum.
It is hushed, and quiet as a wake.

A fan clicks overhead.
Couples sip, with nothing more to say.

A young man sits next to his baby,
talking to his minister about his addiction,
his recovery, and being a good man.
"I locked myself in a room, you see."
"I had a choice . . . to end it."
"This baby . . . this close to being an orphan."

He doesn't know where the mom is, you see.

There is no way I can't hear it.
We sit so close.

Sometimes I think of it, COFFEE.
The door swinging into the kitchen,
the out-of-place waitress,
couples with nothing more to say,
the baby's blank eyes,
the fan clicking and coffee cups clanking,
in East Tennessee.

Meat Cooking in Selma

Have you been to Selma? What a disgrace.
Wicked words, want of retreat off this page,
lepers livid with me, hiding their face,
reversing dark time under a rug.

No, not the tender bones of bravery.
No, not the private monument funded
by those that took the beating,
off the side here littered in broken glass.
But yes, the shameful lack of anything, from us.

Four trillion dollars to the national coffers
every March to every March,
irony in the iron,
over sixty years. The ignominy.
No federal monument, not even bricks.
Hush, don't debate,
we have one for the organ pipe cactus
in Arizona for God sake.

Yes, the name is on the metal here, Edmund.
The paint well kept.

You can walk the bridge, over that hump in the cold,

and when you get to the bottom of it
you can stand looking awkward at the weeds
on the strip of asphalt where gas masks swung ash Billys
and Amelia was beaten unconscious by a man.
And on a night like tonight,
in mist and sweet smoke from the pit over there,
under a lit plastic tent with two men huddled in it,
we can smell the cooking.

Then forget, and go on,
on our merry way to Montgomery,
to make it to dinner.

Derivatives of a Bob Dylan Love Song

Sitting in moonlight shining on bronze
limbs of a gumbo limbo,
where manmade lights don't exist,
it is the same—the full moon at middle night.
Lit, the natural world is alive
and you can always see the trees breathing.

Bob Dylan sings
of a woman who can take dark out of nighttime.
The world wonders what this song means:
'The Statue of Liberty.' 'God.' 'Joni Mitchell.'
I wonder what is hunting

along the edge of the beach at this moment,
cruising slow in the dark.
There is pink on the horizon now,
let me grab my shoes and go see.

Pale light on wet green palm.
What is it about pale wet light at dawn?
I've made this walk,
at this moon angle, on this calendar moon,
five years ago,
all hell breaking loose,

one more piece of bad luck away
from ruin—after a lifetime of work.

Speaking of ruin,
I'm walking past a destroyed wooden house,
lit up like a lantern,
light peeking out its canvas tarps,
and I go past it to the beach.

Holy shit.

Not something to say in a poem,
but you can say it in a song,
and this aftermath is a war zone,
and it's true,
and it's gonna be sung.

Twisted drowned mangroves grappling on the ground,
like tangled barbed wire fighting to a death.
Sand dunes piled ten feet high—a no man's land,
a half-sunken chair angled, ready to fire artillery,
boulders split in two and rusted from flame.
It is a wasteland,
and for some reason
there is one small hole on my walk
to the water's edge.
I am the only person for miles,
and moonlight reflects
the top of slow breaching waves,
glittering like diamonds
on the most beautiful flat ocean,
so I play a song,

yep, that one,
and think of running on this beach two decades ago,
with the girls, their curls and dresses
in the nectarine sun,
laughing.

Montana

In the slow bend of this stream where a ripple creek feeds in,
sits a brown trout from heaven who willows in the flow.

Alone on Odell, I slid in below,
my worn hand on my worn handle.

The cold seeped—as it does,
the mud swirled—as it does,
and I dipped on one knee in the tug.

When the bugs in the banks and the swallows in the heather
and the moon in the sky forgot me and carried on,
I raised my graphite,
felt the horsehair and stick of the barb,
and let it swing away.

The red-threaded royal dropped delicate and true,
its olive silhouette drifted pure on the seam.
The sun was at apex, glinting,
piercing a pocket of shadow.

And in the clear at the end of the run
a dark emerged, turning like a buck,
and floated up to sip, and I saw it.

It missed.
Waiting for a beat, I flicked it up again,
smelling mud.

In the slow bend of this stream sits a brown trout
    from heaven
that I held soft in my hands,
that I hold soft in my hands,
who willows in the flow.

I can see the glint.
I can feel the tug,
and I can hear my old man running to see,
his line swaying in the tall grass.

Reuben at the Bluff

I walked Reuben to the bluff in July at midnight. A full
moon backlit the sky of white stratus over Lake Michigan.
Clouds closed swift the one perfect hole in its blanket.
Then, like a lens opening, the hole reappeared, with the
glowing moon in the middle, a white pupil in a black iris.
We stood watching awhile, a dog barked in the shuttered
cottages of the lane, and the sound lingered, and I walked
Reuben home past the coils of the oak grove.

Beans and Meat

A heavy-set young man
with a mask on
and unsavory hair,
tending the counter
at a dim Courtyard Marriott.
Cleveland's west side.

Dinner menu is brutal.
He's coughing,
I'm struggling.
I go for Caesar salad, bourbon chaser.

We chat football.
He shows me a pic,
of a double amputee
he took care of.

He punked this amputee,
a Steelers fan,
merciless by taping pictures
of the Browns where
the amputee couldn't reach.
But they were just having fun,

they were Marines.
The VA fucked up his amputee's surgery,
skin too high or too thin
for the good prosthetics
you can get in Indiana.

You were a Marine?
Yeah.
What years?
'97 to December '01.
During 9/11? Where were you?
California.
Then Ground Zero.
Ground Zero?
Yeah.
What?
Yeah. Digging in the rubble.
What?
Yeah. Volunteered. About ninety of us.
Damn.
Yeah.
I don't dream anymore.
My doctor figured that's my PTSD.
I can't dream at night,
but I can daydream.
Had one two years back.
I was about to undergo a gastric bypass,
and in this daydream
had a vision I would be in the ICU for six months
if I did the surgery.
So I didn't do it.
Sorry to bring up 9/11.

It's OK.
What was it like, Ground Zero?
I met President Bush,
and it was smoking.
That's why I don't drink anymore,
the smell of it.
Reminds me of burning flesh.
Damn.
People don't understand.
I met President Clinton too, in California.
I was setting up chairs,
he was speaking to us.
He said hello to each of us.
He came to me,
my friend asked him to pin
my lance corporal chevrons on me.
Had them in my pocket.
I had been demoted to private.
He pinned them on me.
I wasn't a Bill Clinton fan before,
but I was after.
If a president pins them on you,
they can't take that away,
so I got lance corporal pay
from there on out.
Why the demotion?
My weight.
Your weight?
Yeah.
I was 255.
To get into the corps I had to get to 240.
I did it.

Then got to Parris for training and I went to 165.
After Parris, I went over 185, got demoted.
Couldn't keep that weight.
They sprayed a red line on my shirt.
I'd eat like two eggs,
then put a flak jacket on and do calisthenics.
I would go through the line,
and only eat beans and meat.
I still couldn't hit that weight.

A woman walks up.
Interrupts our chat.
She is upset.
No one is at the front desk.
In fact, she's damn near irate.
He goes and helps her.

Mandalay

Standing in a window half clothed,
high up in Mandalay Bay, Las Vegas,
looking over a concrete field.

I recognize two concrete towers,
and that chain-link fence,
and look up, at gold-reflecting windows,
those gold windows I saw on TV,
floors up from me.
This vantage, this exact vantage,
in Mandalay Bay,
where the shooting happened.

It is dead quiet except a white noise
tunneling through this thick glass like ants working,
automobiles below,
and aircraft engines just beyond.

The hum reminds me of the sound of a night
in the Ritz in Kuala Lumpur,
staring out at twinkling lights.
I can see the blue quilted bedspread in that room,
and my leather shoes on the floor,
one of them on its side resting on the other,

burned in my brain,
because I arrived in the wee hours,
after a twenty-seven-hour trek,
flying in a 777 across the Pacific,
listening to *its* white noise,
then arriving and turning on the TV
in the middle of the night
to the reporting of the Bataclan.

Now again, I'm staring out the window
of a lost city moving below.

When I Walk into an Old Barn of Tools

Walking into an old barn of tools is always a strange thing.
Sawdust hides where a man hung his rope, the logging axe
    waits for him to come back.
Sometimes you know the man. Sometimes you don't.

What was worked on, what was next?
A bench saw,
an open vise.
A pair of boots.
The smell of rubber.
A glass bottle dug up from the field.
A chain hanging from a beam.

Light through the old windows burns a spot. Stiff, dry, tall
    grass knocks against the walls, and the barn timbers
    ache in the blowing wind like a ship straining in the
    night. There was music here. Now the room is frozen
    in the sunlight, like a tree in winter, waiting.

Frontier Newspaper

I sat down to read a frontier newspaper.
From *The Madisonian*, 1914:

Mr. Metzel left for Twin Bridges this morning.

Nolan Lockridge of Cameron auto-ed to Ennis on
Saturday.

Lewis Gilbert is confined to his home this week with a
severe attack of la grippe.

Dr. Southerland amputated the little finger of the left
hand of Charles Cock.

Nick Carey has been in the hills near Granite Creek gath-
ering up cattle from the summer range and expects to
leave with them to Sheridan today.

Miss Sara Lynch of Adobetown was taken to the sanitar-
ium at Warm Springs Wednesday.

Electricity explained. It is obtained from magnets and
other sources of scientific nature.

Caption. Execution of a German spy who was caught by the Belgians near Termonde. He was led out at dawn, blindfolded, and shot.

Died—At Alder, Sunday, October 25, of cholera infantum, the little daughter of Mr. and Mrs. Allen Long, aged three months and seven days.

Frank Tison, an old-timer of this county, died last week at the county farm and internment was made Monday. He was born July 12, 1843, but few details are known concerning his life.

PART II.

WHALING TOWN

Whaling Town

I.

I stand in a whaling town,
looking at a break wall so far,
and I want to lick a knife.

Maybe it's Melville.

I'm in New Bedford,
driving to see jewelry on Acushnet.

Most buildings empty.
Some makeshift and hopeful: 'Guatemalan Rellenitos.'
Some full and somber: 'We buy Gold.'

Ten blocks from St. Anthony, I see what might be.

F O L C O
Jewelers (AGS)
registered jewelers

A 1940s tan rock façade dripping in stains of dirt.
I walk in.
Sweet old Italian couple.

"We've owned it since 1960. What was his name?"

Borkowski.

An old man in headgear walks out, thumbing through a tome.
"What's that book, dear?"
She's never seen it. He doesn't answer.

"Where did he live?" he asks.

86 Nye. He had a studio eight blocks from there.

The man flips to the back, a reverse telephone book he says.
"This wasn't his store. I remember a place as a kid."
"Little cameras in the window. I used to go in. A little guy
    inside."

"How do you remember, dear?"

"Cameras are my passion!"

Gliding his finger down a page, he pauses.

"Marcel?"

Yes.

"1248 Acushnet. That was it. I used to go in there. He was
    a little guy."

I want to have dinner with this couple.

Instead, I drive south down Acushnet,
crawling, and see the marquee, rusted.

FREMS
Jewelry

No longer his name, but his place.
I know by the two-story tenement on top.
It's how he made his way, collecting rent, door to door.

The light inside is dim like a museum in a lonely place,
paneled wood, nooks and crannies, brown.
I feel him alone here, working,
long ago taking pictures of fellow immigrants.
I've never been here, but I have.
A picture hangs in my house
of my sister and me in lederhosen,
taken in this room fifty years ago, by Dadziu.

A young couple peeks in, then walks in, and asks,
"What's the pink stone in the window?"
Dunno, this was my great-grandfather's place.

I walk to the back. A makeshift room.
Had to be his darkroom.

On my way out, breathing it all in fast,
I hear the owner say, "We don't take pawn,"
and the couple leans heavy on the glass.

I head up to St. Anthony, walking his path home.
Polish signs gone.

Portuguese signs few.
Central Americans' signs new,
and a man on the corner is selling lawn ornaments
from the back of his van
of Chucky and Mario and bulldogs.

At Nye and Acushnet, it is calm,
and I walk up the steps of St. Anthony,
red and rusted, daunting and European.
The doors are locked. I go to the side.
A surveillance sign says 'be back soon.'
I walk around and run into a food-pantry line
of all colors and new shapes,
from Acushnet all the way to a yellow house
near the unloading of pallets of food.
He lived on the first floor of this yellow house,
with Zosh and Mudder and Linda, my mother.

I send a pic.
"Yes, that was it," Linda replies.
"The kids played in the churchyard.
If their balls came across the street, Dadziu would often
    confiscate them."

You see, I met him a couple times.
Reel-to-reel clips in my head.
Once I splashed water on him, and he was not happy.
He did not speak English to me.
One more memory,
purple plastic drapes in a room filled with smoke.

He came from East Poland at twenty,

after his family was shot, after the Great War.
There was not a lot of small talk, and that was fine with me.
What I did know as a child,
he knew his debits and credits,
and he made sense.

II.

A lady in a gown is at the back door of the church.
"Hello? Did you ring the bell?"

Yes.

She leads me into the cathedral,
dipping her hands in holy water.
I confess I'm not Catholic, so no dip.

"You can stay and take pictures."

I won't be long.

St. Anthony in New Bedford
is St. Peter's in a whaling town in America.
I walk to the altar under its towering saints,
and sit on cracking wood in the first pew.
I say a prayer. I'm not sure what, but I do,
and listen for God.

I hear it.

Sirens outside.

St. Anthony's bells.
Ringing in a whaling town.
Sirens and food lines.

III.

I crane my neck to see the organ pipes
and walk out into fading fall light,
and turn to my hotel by the water.

Early this morning a captain in front of his boat *Rebecca*,
with a rusted wheelchair strapped to the deck,
told me in a Portuguese accent,
"That was long ago. The whale ships used Pier 3."

I walk Pier 3 now.

Santa Maria
Jenna Lee
Quincy 2
Elizabeth Katherine
Temptress
Growler
Seawolf
Beth Ann

Halogen lights hang in metal rigging,
in the droll of diesel in this working harbor,
at the mouth of the Acushnet River on Buzzards Bay.

This is a place you never hear about in America,
but to these cobbles he came.
The city that lit the world.

Of course. Of course, here.
He came for freedom and work and to escape death,
selling on the street.

Today a Central American sells lawn ornaments
fifty steps from where my Polish great-grandfather
sold pictures a hundred years earlier.
Both of 'em coming to a city, a system,
a people, and a country that lights the world.

This dream is not fading.
Far from it.
The people doing the bleeding write this story.

Strolling down the harbor,
past pilings and phosphor-lit gulls,
I think,
I would not be walking if not for you, Dadziu.

PART III.

"May we light the fire of Nachiketa."

Katha Upanishad III.1.1

Staring Contest with a Blackbird

A blackbird sits on a brown spike of a cattail in spring,
    in a marsh.
He is velvet black, with a red burn on his wing
    as red as African ochre.
His outfit is sharp,
    a tuxedo just cleaned and pressed and donned.

"Hello, your majesty."

I am still, so still I feel my pupils expand.
His left eye stares at me.
My two eyes stare at him.
No movement.
Like all wild animals, if you stare
they will move once they decide they are bored,
think it best to retreat or decide to attack.

OK, Mr. Blackbird,
I am content to stay here for a very long time.

Let me use telepathy to move you off.
Let me tell you how we humans are running this world
    and tire you off.
Let me tell you how to make blackbird stew and run you off.

I notice my breath has run out.
He has won.
I move.
He sits in the marsh in spring.

In the Dark Wood I Spotted

In the dark wood I spotted a stage of moonlit snow.
Upon it was my shadow in a shape I admit I know.
Now the human shadow, look and note how tame
next to the shape of an elk, or a ragged dog with no name.

Beasts have edges.
Beasts have gait.
Beasts are made for stalking with fangs not made for hate.

There is a day a man must weigh the tin his pack contains.
For it is all he has.

With spit dripping and neck aching with the bent aspens,
my legs buckled,
"I cannot outrun the sun."
I looked in the mirror and thought,
Jesus, I haven't looked at myself in . . .

I lifted the veil and said, "All you see is all there is."
Good.
I licked the salt on my lips.

Yes, my crate is stamped on the wharf.
Yes, how do I explain Lippmann, "the pictures in their heads."

If you don't believe me,
pick up a river rock from the bed of a stream and look
    under it.

I did and lifted it from its cage.
Then I fluttered over to the bush and sat in it naked.
I raised my face to the rain. It melted me in the stream.
I submerged and disassembled and found it not a dream.

Nocturnal Mountain Road

I see lantern beams coming up a gravel mountain road, searching in the dark. Inside, it is quiet but for the low rumble of gravel and the shaking of plastic and glass and metal. The driver is hanging on, staring ahead, like a pilot in turbulence over a dark sea.

He will pass two glowing eyes in the ditch. Then he will make the turn near the old schoolhouse, wheeling onto the flat. In his tunnel vision of spot-white light ahead, surrounded by black, a deer will appear from nowhere, standing, nibbling in the middle of the dirt road, illumed in the beam. It will look up in a frozen pause and its nocturnal eyes will stare straight into him, and the nanosecond before he can move the wheel, the deer, as a dancer on a stage, will dip and torque and bolt three quick lunges, and he will see its hind muscles tighten as it hinges, and then leap four feet in the air, sailing effortless over the barb into the black.

The driver will continue up the flat, zoned out in the rumble, and will see the light on in the house up the way, and he is dreading pulling in and sharing the news he received down below.

Song for Charlie Patton

I found your grave listing in a floodplain
next to this railroad track you walked.

I'm standing six feet above you,
your sockets and teeth now looking up at me,
your pickin' hands so close I can touch.

There is cotton up here, Charlie,
blowin' like tumbleweeds,
stragglers of the harvest across the Delta.
It is so quiet up here, flat, and dry.

I met a farmer with five thousand acres up near Sunflower.
He told me about flood irrigation,
and the horses that stood on the tracks in the '27 flood.
He said labor is hard these days, and there was a silence.
But you know all about that.

I went to your plantation where you played with Willie
    and Son,
and saw the iron well you drank lip to lip with the mules,
next to the cotton gin. I walked inside it, those metal pipes.
I walked the road south out of there too,
over the bridge of that milky clay-green river.

Tracking the Sunflower at night must have been
     somethin'.

Listen, Charlie, thank you for the chants and the voice
     and the beats.
There is a truck comin' and I feel I am trespassing on a
     graveyard
in my white skin, but I know you understand,
and I wanted to tell you face to face,
your music and your wailin' . . .

So long, Charlie.

Over This Lonesome Field

In a hot-stripped cotton field in the Delta,
young after harvest, vapor is moving low
across the ground and finds a shaft of cool.
Dust, this hypnotized snake,
rises and begins to twist,
gathering wide,
up and up,
spreading its arms like a crucifix rising
firm against the wind,
and then, charged electric,
does its dervish dance over the dry dirt,
and we watch specks of dried cotton bolls
rise and spin slow in a trance,
aware,
over this lonesome field.

When I Wet the Lips of Death

I know the time comes,
I wet the lips of death, smelling
fresh paint on your breath.

Roaring '20s

You can hear it in 'Stardust',
the swing of the head,
the flash of Lucille's eyes,
dancing,
trumpet buzzing,
no glimmer of the past,
of a four-year-old thrown to the floor in the dark,
waking to her mother
running up the stairs on fire,
then sitting in that Baptist church three days later with
    Daddy.

Tonight it is just 'Stardust',
the brassy timbre of now.

I See Headlights Coming

I see headlights coming.
Little specks of moth grains floating in the low beams.
In the past they came slow and steady.
Tonight tires roll, rise, and sink in sand dunes.

I stand outside a gate with one door missing.
No crunch of shell, just the hum of heat
from an engine slowing to a stop.
The window rolls down.
I see the soft pearl face of nine decades.
She knows the epic of a flood, but it's been a while.
"Hi, honey," she says, lonesome as an orphan.

They've lived here sixty years, the home they built.
Tomorrow we will go out and visit it, the destruction.

Imagine you are in a tsunami, a rag doll
barreling for sharp wood pikes in the sand.
You are in a Cat 5 and have drawn a bad angle,
and you can do nothing but let the violence come.

I will spare you the details, except this one.

There is a gull hopping on one leg in a dead bush
next to steps that head up to a frame of blown-out windows.
I hold your elbow and you peek in.
The bedroom is a pool of oil-black water,
the water surrounds your bed three inches from the top,
the lace pillows are still made neat,
and floating in the water is the rest of it.
I take your soft arm. You step off.

We sit next door, up high this night,
in candlelight,
listening to Coltrane float on 'In a Sentimental Mood'
in the open doors, eating noodles with pepper,
smelling the Areca palm that will come back,
sitting in the quiet languid pace of this island,
a heaven on earth.

In the Din of the Plunging Breakers

I woke to a dark.
When it is early morning alone
on a barrier island in the Gulf,
your mind counts quick the seconds it takes to hit water.

My feet hit the floor.

The screen door was open in the kitchen.
The surf was up, landing thuds.
The smell of sweet salt sifted in the room
with the kicking of a breeze.

I put a small glass votive candle
and a box of matches in my pocket (why, I don't know).
I brewed espresso and felt for the thin
porcelain handle of my chipped cup.

I walked out the back door and inhaled,
closing the sturdy latch behind.

A snook light on the neighbor's house illumed
the banyan on the sandy lane.
I walked invisible down the middle,
and thought of clocks and couples sipping tea.

I turned into the mangrove tunnel.
The decibel of the surf rose in stride,
and I came to the weathered wooden step,
felt for the splinters on the rail,
and my bare feet landed in chilled night sand.

I rested the votive on the armchair,
breathed in, then exhaled into the space,
and leaned back to contemplate nothing,
in the din of the plunging breakers.

I thought about it, and so I did it.
I walked the votive to the edge of the wash,
cupped it as you would a dove,
lit a match in the wind,
and set the fragile glass in the sand.

I sat down to watch,
this little light, flickering in front
of six hundred and forty-three quadrillion
gallons in the Gulf gusting twenty knots,
the force in fathoms and depths insane.

I rose to retrieve it, reaching down.
The candle listed like a shipwreck,
sunken, stuck and lit, in the ground.
I blew out the flame and walked back home in the dark.

Standing in the kitchen minutes later
reminded me of Charlotte's kitchen,
and in the grey light I spotted a still life on the counter,
casting a shadow of an old woman hunched on the stone.

Ocean Lung

The ocean, a lung
heaving up and down,
exhausted, from us.

The Autopsy of Oscar Parker

A small brain.
Crooked teeth.
A scar over the left eye.
Some bones slight.
Stalagmites in the kidneys.
Fat lips with a pearl mass in the lower.
Blue eyes, pupils ringed with olive.
One rib concave.
A comet-shaped mole on the right little toe.
Stubby hands.
A bright liver.
Calves for pushing an oxcart in mud.
A faded bite mark on the meat of the left hand.
Feet bones worn like fossils in a rock.
Heart 128 grams.
Blood with hints of currant and cherry.
A slight smile in rigor mortis.

The accounting is that Oscar Parker had four traits worth
    scientific note out of the typical human seventy-eight
    organs, two hundred bones, and nine hundred liga-
    ments, equating to a zero-point-three percent rate

worth Aristophanes's study. The traits of note: fat-scarred lips, spiced blood, adapted feet, and a feather heart weighed by Anubis on Maat's scale.

Birth of a Tragedy

My life has begun,
a puddle of rainwater
cursing finite time
praying for more rain.

Speaking of one's life,
Nietzsche has a thought.
Live as if every minute will repeat itself.
Don't be fooled, this is worth a study.

Ripples in the puddle.
Ripples in this poem.

What are we after all,
Evaporating?
Why has this been,
holding on?
Building thatches in storms.
Picking up pieces.
Basking in fleeting sun.

Standing over the puddle with my arms behind my back,
curious in its watery white reflection,
I see a horse's eye weeping,

black, endless, telepathic.
Rawhide, turning slow,
then walking into the field,
nipping at grass before night.

Love Tape, Eject

At the crosswalk,
an orange neon hand says stop.
Stop! appeasing people with bad intentions.
Stop! your vanity.
Stop! being naïve the world is kind.
Let that bus go by with forty souls and not one smile.
Wake up.
Tell her you love her.

Now walk.
Crossing a gum-stained street,
remembering the pleasant feeling
of hitting the eject button on the tape recorder so hard,
remember that!
The plastic Maxell tape.
Under a Blood Red Sky
would come flying out,
bouncing on the wood floor.

And then we ran outside in the streets of Prague,
over that misty bridge.

Or was it sun.

Here in the Fjord, High in the Fjord

I see a fleck of sage gilded in granite,
soft, exposed, and free.
My fingers feel for brail on this black plateau.
Here in the fjord, high in the fjord,
I must let it go.

I see a plume of pine, silent in green,
weeping on the slope.
A wood house sits still in the field alone.
Here in the fjord, high in the fjord,
I must let it go.

Veins plunge vertical gouges to the deep.
Water falls distant near a spot of snow.
The sun burns a gasp on the far side of the hill.
Here in the fjord, high in the fjord,
I must let go.

I held your hand today. I held you close today.
Here in the fjord, high in the fjord,
and with my last breath,
daughter,
I let you go.

Fire and Ice

She left home several years ago.
Now I'm driving down to meet her
before she goes back to her new home,
the Bronx,
with her scalpel.

The city towers sit in a cauldron
of fire in the rising east sun,
and I have one goal for the morning,
to say little.
Soak in the time.
Not talk politics.
Not say something stupid.

Over breakfast in a grocery store
she tells of her patients and their fears.
Some don't speak English,
her hospital's funding is being threatened,
and the kids take their passports to school
in case of an ICE raid.

I didn't understand in November
why the degree of her concern.
I tried to tell her . . . now, now . . . there, there,
who would hurt a little girl?

Me, the man who moved her when she was fourteen.
Me, the man who barked at her more
than the service dog I said not to get,
the one that saved her life.

Daughter

Daughter, strong daughter,
why are you so mad
at me. I didn't, I didn't
say the words you say I said.
Or did I.
Not in my head, but in my face and voice,
a varmint I cannot see.

Fathom, I can't fathom,
but you I believe.
I need to go for a walk,
and paint a self-portrait,
of a rain-soaked fisherman with wrinkled eyes
in a navy-blue oilskin hat,
walking in the door,
dripping in droplets,
about to say,
Daughter, I miss you,
let's go walk in the rain.

Room 703

Early-morning sun is shining in 703.
A faded yellow diary sits on a blue love seat
and dust floats down in the light.
"Good morning, dear," Ruth says.

She looks across Sixty-Fifth Street.
A couple's life is spread in view.
A woman walks hurried in the bedroom.
A man walks aimless in the kitchen.

"You should've seen the stars, dear."

Walking to the kitchen she wonders,
What day is today?

Saturday.

"Let's sit down for coffee, dear," pulling out her chair.
"Today is the big move."
"Audrey is coming, and the bellman."

The chair across is half in, half out.
The grandfather clock ticks and chimes,
melancholy if you are alone
or alive if you have company.

An alabaster pamphlet sits on the table
under saltshakers with tin tops,
and reads,
'In Loving Memory of Sam Willowby.'

The bell rings.
Ruth rises and presses the intercom.

I Got You Babe

For hours, a blue weather system
has been moving up the Madison Valley
from the south, a deep ultramarine blue,
under a cloud tower so mighty
it is now a cumulonimbus.
That anvil coming.

Southern wind is a different thing.
Not the chilled disdain of an east,
nor the brutal blow of a north,
less distant than a west,
it is curious and methodic and does the work close.

But this is late winter, and I am high on the bench
of this mountain slope
and there will be no lightning,
and I go to greet it.

I hike up the old game trail behind this homestead,
to the top of the plateau.
With Black Mountain to my east,
I scan fifty miles in three directions
and lock eyes on the south.

This storm is of the massive kind.
Dark rain ribbons fall ten miles away there,
water vapor runs one mile away here,
and sun shines in the center of its wheel
in a white-orange-pink surrounded by this blue.
And like a god with a staff pointing down
riding this storm chariot, the trumpets are blowing now
forty knots, I let the cold wind wash and sting my face,
and looking down, there is a vine with red leaves
blowing back, hanging on in bent mercy,
and somehow it has made it through winter.

As the wind passes, I watch the mixture drift north,
then turn my gaze back south from where it came.
The cottonwoods below me haven't moved.
They are still, twisted and bent like dancing women
with bare limbs frozen in place, in leaning poses
over the slow, black creek water flowing by.

I walk back down the game trail of the cut,
looking for tracks in the yellow wet grass.
And Stephanie is waiting for me there,
and I have disappointed her.

Thirty years of marriage will do that to you,
osmosis,
knowing that I have explaining to do,
and this one better be good.
So before I say a word, I go back in time,

back to stanza six.

As the wind passes, I watch the mixture drift north,
then turn my gaze back south from where it came.
The cottonwoods below me haven't moved.
They are still, twisted and bent like dancing women
with bare limbs frozen in place, in leaning poses
over the slow, black creek water flowing by.

I look and see her, Stephanie,
walking up the trail by herself in bear country,
where the grizzlies are soon to leave their dens,
and I hightail it.

Thawing

Cicadas under our feet,
sucking on roots.

Who is it thinking?
A mind looks out.
Why is it thinking?
The Branta fly north.

And in the green-grey fog
on the dawn of the new moon,
a figure emerges down the street,
a dark lumber, swaying.

The thing about images in fog,
there is movement in stillness,
an undercurrent in slowing time,
but we're not slowing down.

We rocket one million miles an hour
oblivious in our earth cocoon.
Watching this man cross Scranton Avenue
on my little walks around the block for twenty years.
I don't know his name.

Who is breathing?
The lichen in the tundra.
What is breathing?
The permafrost, gasping.

I'll Meet You at the Swing

'I'll meet you at the swing,'
says the ink on the note, sitting on the desk,
written in your hand.

I can tell by the way
your strokes are quick and curve
you want me to join you,
watching the water-ouzel
dip and bob up the stones,
dunking its head,
splashing in the stream.

You sit and swing,
smile and think,
giggling at this bird,
blissful,
looking at the mountains we share.

I walk to you,
watching your hair in the sun,
your wrists exposed,
and I think of them as I walk,
despising them,
the times I've let you down.

The wind in the cottonwood blows.
I can feel you on a string,
sharp as a razor,
and my brain is filled with water.

Will you die in my arms?
Or will it be me?
I cannot bear the thought of it,
but it is a gift, and I walk numb.

I Hope I Don't Expire Unexpected

I hope I don't expire unexpected,
because there are things in my closet
I hope not be found.

The reminder I did not do,
your gift I did not wear,
Jo's little collar with her name on it,
the note I kept,
my words I did not share.
The bible I haven't opened
next to a copy of *A Farewell to Arms*,
and you will wonder why it is there,
and there is no reason.
The smooth rungu from the Mara, my only weapon,
a club, in my drawer of drawers waiting,
this at least will make you laugh,
me the warrior.

I think of you looking at my empty worn leather shoes,
and my old bag of shoe polish,
the sound of tins hollow-knocking when you pick it up,
and I realize
I haven't kissed you goodbye.

Eat Your Heart Out

I'm so tired of giving a shit my kidneys hurt.
I need to take a walk.
Hon, let's go take the plunge.
We walk to it, but I don't go in.
I'm not man enough for that.
But she is.

I watch you walk into Lake Michigan doing your little
    shoulder dance,
the sun's low angle burns gold your skin,
the water fifty-three degrees on a blue October day.
You wade up to your neck, far out, and I hear you exhale,
me standing downwind in the ice water up to my shins.
You turn like a little girl on a merry-go-round,
I make out your smile when you look at me.
The water laps the boulders,
and a ladybug struggles to fly, catching its last rays.

Rectangles of tall towers, the skyline, sixty miles below.
Are you thinking about our daughter down there?
Let me guess what you are thinking:
the Mediterranean dish I want you to make me for dinner.

Here you come, Bo Derek.

Opening your arms to the sun,
"Eat your heart out," you say.

'Eat your heart out' . . . it's an odd saying, no?

I get your towel and wrap it around your shoulders.

"What were you thinking out there, babe?"
I already know the answer because I'm a 'man' after all,
and I can't wait for this dinner, but I ask anyway.

She says,
"I should probably swim laps."

We turn and walk together,
and I bite my lip as we walk slow out of the sand.

ACKNOWLEDGMENTS

Whaling Town started in a hotel room in Monterey, California, on April 4, 2023, as a song called Miss Fortune, which is not in this book. Why I wrote and sung it into my phone in the middle of that night, I don't know.

A week later I was in Houston and called a long-time friend living there to bring his guitar to my hotel. We cut a rough demo of the song. It was the first time I told a story into a guitar, and I wasn't sure it would work. I had written bits of fiction for many years, but my life had other priorities, including coming out of a period in which I risked and faced the possibility of losing everything too late in life to lose everything. Along with the almighty Gravity, staring into an abyss forces decisions on ultimate questions, and I started looking at the world a little different.

By Fall 2023 I had a batch of songs. While researching them, I took a trip to the Mississippi Delta to trace the steps of Charley Patton. Born in the late 1800s, Patton is regarded as one of the earliest blues pioneers. When I found his music out on that floodplain, it floored me. The rhythm of his beats and phrasing, like what W. C. Handy first heard in 1903 on a bench at the tiny train platform in Tutweiler, MS, led me down the path of studying the melodic beats of the early blues writers—men and women discovered when the field recordings came to the deep south in the 1920s. As I dug deeper into those roots and compositions, this led me to the preceding lyrical verse written across the pond a couple hundred years prior, and then back to the folk songs and hymns that spread into the hills, plains and mountains of rural America from the 1820s—1930s as America moved west. In doing so, I unexpectedly found poetic verse (poetry) and immersed myself in trying to become a skilled free verse writer.

This is not a political book. *Whaling Town* is part memoir, part observation. To that end, it is hard for me not to notice what is going on in the world and not say something about it. A lot has been said by great writers. The world doesn't need the same things said. *Whaling Town* is a collection cut down from ninety poems, and I decided to publish it as I realized the places and people had something to say. For me at least, it's the truth.

I want to thank my family and friends, and most of all my wife Stephanie. When she said the words, "Til death do us part," she didn't know she was signing up for this. I want to thank the American poet Matthew Lippman for his encouragement and candid coaching on the craft of writing, and Steve Rashid, an Emmy-winning composer and talented musician and producer who did not need to take on my project accompanying *Whaling Town*. I also want to thank the team at Girl Friday Productions for bringing this book to life.

Last, I owe so much to those that came before me, my grandparents whom I was lucky to know, who lived in hard times but worked steadfast and with great faith and love, and who told me their stories. Stories of making ends meet, of strong men and strong women, of tragedies, of fires, of floods, of pandemics, of depressions, of fine and funny characters, of the land in rural America, of battles and wars, of trips around the world, of families, of bad luck and good luck, of faith and of living the American dream.

ABOUT THE AUTHOR

DAVID PARKER ALLEN is an American songwriter, poet, and entrepreneur. *Whaling Town* is his first published prose poetry collection, and he is currently recording his first country blues folk album. He splits his time between Chicago and the Gulf Coast of Florida.